Waiting for Godot's First Pitch

Waiting for Godot's First Pitch

More Poems from Baseball

TIM PEELER

To John Howard —
The waiting is the
hardest part.

Tim Peeler
8-16-13

McFarland & Company, Inc., Publishers
Jefferson, North Carolina, and London

ALSO BY TIM PEELER

Touching All the Bases: Poems from Baseball
(McFarland, 2000)

Acknowledgments

The author wishes to thank the following publications in which some
of these poems first appeared: *Spitball*: "The Grass Is Green";
The Dead Mule School of Southern Literature: "In This Keen Light";
Black Bear Review: "The Intrusion of Snakes" and "Temple America";
Elysian Fields Quarterly: "Pepi Played the Game Like a Tune" and "In Outlaw Tales";
Main Street Rag: "Drowning Lessons."
Many of these poems first appeared as regular contributions
to the *Enteractive Weekly*.
Thanks, Dave.

LIBRARY OF CONGRESS CATALOGUING-IN-PUBLICATION DATA

Peeler, Tim, 1957–
    Waiting for Godot's first pitch : more poems from
baseball / Tim Peeler.
        p.   cm.
    Includes index.

    ISBN 0-7864-1127-9 (softcover : 50# alkaline paper)

    1. Baseball—Poetry.   I. Title.
PS3566.E276 W35   2001
811'.54—dc21   2001041031

British Library cataloguing data are available

Front cover: ©2001 Wood River Gallery

Manufactured in the United States of America

McFarland & Company, Inc., Publishers
Box 611, Jefferson, North Carolina 28640
www.mcfarlandpub.com

For the teachers—
Leon Lewis and Janette Sims
For the coaches—
Frank Eller and J.L. Peeler
For the sons—
Aaron Michael and Thomas Dylan Peeler

Contents

Preface

People often leave their homes in search of another place that, on some level, reminds them of where they came from. Writers, too, follow a search through ideas and through the corridors of stories that ultimately lead them back to their origins. In late August of 1998, I finished what would be the final additions to my first book of baseball poems. And though I'd labored at the start, the material, drawn mostly from memories of adolescence and fortified by a bit of baseball mythology, soon rose unbidden from my past, seeming to ease itself onto the page. I had tapped a creative vein, as some say, and, encouraged, I tended the flue for long hours and with zeal. I had found my way to the poetic niche that had waited for me through years of creative struggle, self-doubt, and misdirected effort.

The publication of *Touching All the Bases* proved, itself, a rich mine of opportunity. My work has reached more interested readers than I ever thought possible. As a result of that book, I have met and begun friendships with several unique individuals that I must mention: bookseller and quintessential entrepreneur Robert Canipe; venerable baseball researcher and historian Hank Utley; ever youthful rock 'n' roll musician Robert Kearns (Chris Duarte Group); and, of course, baseball literature aficionado Gary Mitchem.

In addition, the audiences I've read for have been both gracious and challenging, strengthening my belief that poetry should be celebrated in a vocal format. Surely there is no better barometer for the success of a poem than a live sudience. My reading experiences over the past year have proved their value, pushing me toward new work that often appeals first to the ear.

W.P. Kinsella has noted that "a baseball player is only as good as his last 50 at-bats," and "an author is only as good as his last book." And let me tell you, having found myself in the comfy recesses of my own little creative gold mine, there was no way I could stop writing baseball poems (and still can't). By early 1999, I realized that *Touching All the Bases* would be more a milepost than a milestone for me.

Waiting for Godot's First Pitch began in a hotel room high above an ugly Detroit winter day in February 1999. Suffering from strep throat and an elevated fever, I scribbled the beginnings of the abstract title piece. What began as a sort of diary of baseball poems soon became a 20-month project. I wrote, rewrote, added, and eliminated, revising to greater effect than I believe I ever have and finding formal strictures more useful. The final product reflects what fit best together both thematically and stylistically.

These pages, like those of *Touching All the Bases*, are filled with people and recollections from my past, as well as considerations of baseball heroes, both present-day and historical. But the territory, for all its similarity to places my verse has taken me, appears, and so must be, either foreign or wholly grown over. With time, I suppose, even old, familiar geography is home to new creatures.

As I come to the beginning of this volume, I must offer heartfelt thanks for the support of friends at Catawba Valley Community College, Bethlehem Lutheran Church, and the local reading and sports community. For invaluable conversations, I must thank the eminent likes of Johnny Bolick, Bill Baird, Larry Hollar, Dave Hefner, and Terry Saine. For the same and more, I must thank J.L. Peeler, my father, and my sons, Aaron and Thomas, and my father-in-law, Enoch Abernethy. For always keeping things properly focused, yet never doubting that the windmills were real, I am indebted to my wife, Penny. Finally, for teaching me the art of storytelling, I offer these poems to the memory of Cooke Calvin Mull.

Tim Peeler
Hickory, North Carolina
June 2001

There Was a Place We'd Go
After the Baseball Games

Sprung from the traps of gorgeous stone buildings
At the Protestant junior college halfway up
A valley between blue, wispy gray mountains,
A wild gang of us went after the baseball games
To a grassy green hillside where the train
Slammed through a dark tunnel,
And curved into uncertain darkness.

Fresh air took the reek of cheap wine,
Beer spilt on the lush ground—
The team captain alligator rolled
Down the ivy-covered hill to
A drunken cursing heap at the bottom.
Then it happened, a distant whistle,
And a generation trained to act
At the insistence of bells
Leaped to the gravel bed where the moonlight
Pealed down the rails—
We entered the mouth of the tunnel
And stood, erect,
Our backs flattened against the cement wall
As the vibration from the train
Unsettled the ground beneath our feet.
A few players still wore metal cleats;
You could hear them,
Nervously stirring the gravel
As the earth began to shake
And the engine blasted into the tunnel,
Driving its blinding light before it.
The wheels clanked and clanked
Crossing the raised pilings
Near the entrance
While the "iron horse" passed
Like a ferocious rhinoceros
A foot from our chalky faces.

FIRST HIT

My dad so proud to tell everyone
How his "strikeout son" hammered
That grounder up the Pee Wee middle
Past the grazing six-year-old fielders,
Then of the fierce flat out circle
Round the loaded bases, through
Parental screams and the dizzy buzz
Of unconscious accomplishment,
Chlorine wafting from the pool nearby
And the fresh scent of June grass on a
Muggy Carolina afternoon.
Clerical-collared Dad, the beaming
Minister of pride. We would stop
For a rare Coke later
When the Glory died down a bit,
And he could work out
His divine exaggeration.

♦ ♦ ♦ ♦

THE GRASS IS GREEN

And the first tulips are brightly upturned gloves
Of cadmium yellow and two brilliant shades of red,
The differing temperatures of a fire.
I want to repose on the porch in a rocker,
Watch everything grow and bloom
And rise and cradle precious raindrops.
But the grass is a dark new green,
And the hitters are ahead of the pitchers.
And I have always been a pitcher.

Dusting Off the Plate of the Moon

The magnificent December one hovers
Above the slope of eastern sky; money
Rules the day game, but here, when a cloud sssslides
Over the yellow dish, and the wind tips
The hats of the pines gently, the seats are
Free on my front porch, unobstructed, too.

◆ ◆ ◆ ◆

Waiting for Godot's First Pitch

Above,
The husky blue sky
Is a blank face of canvas—
Not even a jet tail
To trace a whisper
Against the silence
Below,
The strain of anthem
Segued to cheer
And throaty organ notes,
Then,
That jungle hush
As the fat blackbird of ump
Notes the glove fit
Of his plump form
Against the stocky catcher's squat—
As this world waits
On the long ice of the moment,
In the lanky pitcher's
Nervous hand,
The first pitch imagines
A blinding path toward the plate.

Looking for My Bumble Bee

Retired Judge Ferrell, comfortable
In his graduation robe, told us when
He spoke at ours about walking in
The backyard with his young grandson, a bright
Eager boy who skipped along chanting
Bumble-bumble-bumble bee, and You know,
Said the judge in a carefully practiced
Oratory, Everyone should try to find
Their bumble bee, and though I wasn't one
Who was graduating, I knew what he
Meant and knew the urge to chase what stings us
If we catch it. The bright buzzing colors,
The sweet allure of dangerous beauty, —
Just to chase a thing that is different
Or strange or meaningful to me and no-one else
I have run up and down
Mountains, through red mud and rocky, broken
Trail beds, in and out of parks and ball parks,
Watching my watch for a reason, month in-
To month till every season became
The season of the bumble bee, and I
Suddenly realized I had become
The casual thing that I hunted.

Looking Homeward

For Jackie Robinson

With all your heart yearning through the white heat,
Looking homeward, your foot leaning on first,
Crossover, stutter and measure, thinking
Of second, blinking the dust away; squint
For a second in afternoon light, stop.
For there is a time to steal and a time
To wait, to ponder goals, breaking them down
Into shorter lengths of success, never
Letting too much of the rope out.

The roar
That chases the bat's sharp explosion
Fires your pistons to third where another
White hand halts your melody and you
Anchor back to the bag—

Back muscles and hamstrings contract
As you stretch calmly
And raise your worshiping face to the sun.

Gathering everything you carry,
You lock your eyes on the plate.

A DRYSDALE WARNING IN EFFECT

You better have your head on your shoulders
When you step to the plate, the Say Hey Kid
Included; no trick of the mind can save
Your noggin if you forget and dig in.

You better wake up before you get up
If you follow your finger down the sports
Page, to find my name listed for your game.
Sandy grants you space, fears his own white blaze,

But not this Dodger, blue-blooded, ready
To blast you with my stormy ammunition.
Don't say you weren't warned—I'm buying later,
                              Should you make it.

◆ ◆ ◆ ◆

TOMMY TIME

At the only fine hotel in town, what
Celebs came to Hickory in the late
Eighties, came to us at the Holiday.

Always surprised at their sheer frequency,
I watched them cross the Georgian marble tile,
Duck into the green clutches of the Piedmont
Park restaurant or simply hover behind
While some rattled little peon dealt with the
Mere desk clerk of me; other guests sauntered
Over to ask, "Was that Reggie?" "What's Bobby
Knight doin' hyere in Hickree?"
"Is that fat dude Meatloaf? That tall feller—
Kristoferson? Was that really Lou Holtz?"

Most of the stars confused you with the wallpaper,
And "they" were nothing more than conversation
Pieces, improbable boasts at late night parties.
That's what I thought till the quiet Friday
When I looked up from a reservation
At a medium-built silver-haired man—
Uncomfortable but pleasant in a loose gray suit,
Shifting his weight as if used to more of it—
"Room for Lasorda," he said, looking about
At the hundred-thousand-dollar wall hangings,
The chandeliers and generally well-appointed
Elegance of the place. We talked about the place
While I checked in his SlimFastness. He spoke
Like I was another human as I
Ignored the ringing phone—and never once mentioned
Kirk Gibson's crippled truck-driver gallop
Around the bases a few years back, or
Fernando and Orel or any
Way-back greats he may have known—though I
Thirsted for stories to pump up the pages
Of my nearly secret baseball poems;
He was too clearly nice to bother, I suppose.
Five, ten minutes he chatted, then, unescorted,
Headed for his room—and I turned back
To the worries of grad school and a family.

What celebs came to Hickory in the eighties
Stayed with us, their frequency surprising—
Twelve years since, I've forgotten them all
But one.

The Last Game at Ebbets Field

Damp, cold New York September,
Seven thousand witnesses,
Danny McDevitt pitching
A 2–0, five-hit shutout
At "the end of something great."

Pee Wee, Snider, and Erskine
Knew the thing was over, could
Not just have a beer and go
Home.

When the Red Sea refilled,
The Dodgers would be long gone,
Their memories driven hard
Like horses and chariots
Away.

How God Watches Baseball

Saturday afternoon run, an April day, cold and bright
Like Orwell's freaky opening—
Taking the rock strewn ridge of Baker's Mountain
Out toward the communications tower,
I watch down and off east where Huffman Park
Huddles beyond the Coca-Cola paint of its buildings;
The outfield fence signs are dazzling colors,
Unreadable from here, like a painter's palette laid
Out in a strip;
The players I know are Little Leaguers
Could be men for what my eyes say,
And the game doesn't move at all
As I climb toward the southern corner;
It is like passing a parked train
Wondering who's moving? them or me?

From here there are no balls and strikes,
No fear of wild pitches,
No psycho coaches screaming sarcasm
At grade schoolers,
No second guesses or venomous parents
Touting their little heroes,
No heroes.

THE GREATEST GIFT EVER

My dad never made more than 17K
In a working year, never took us to a
Fancy restaurant—a country preacher
Is what he was, and he taught me the art
Of pitching, the art of taking things within
My reach and making them work, the art of
Steadiness, the lesson of the tortoise
And the virtue of risk.

My dad never made more than 17K
But he dabbled in the market, and we
Learned pitches together, kept up with the
Fine print of quotes and followed their flow through
The seasons like the pitcher who paces him-
self, holding back for the dog days of late
Summer, holding back for the harvest of
Stubborn strikeouts that surely would come.

My dad never made more than 17K
In a working year, never lavished birthday
Gifts or Christmas presents, never worried
About the money he didn't have or
Could have made, and every summer day
He gave us the greatest gift in the side yard
Between snowball bushes and cherry trees,
Behind a dingy home plate he'd cut from

Plywood, he crouched with a mitt to teach us,
By catching, the art of pitching.

A Sacrament Is What It Was

The backyard mound was the home of my nerves;
My Dad, the shrink that saved my ego with
A wide practice plate. In model faith,
This man who preached every Sunday would
Perch himself on the thatch stool my older
Brother wove from straw for a Boy Scout badge,
And Approve as I zipped heat through heat
And red dust spit up on his black shoes and
Black socks and white bruised legs. Sometimes, reaching
For a slow curve, his back spasmed, seized by
A ghost I've come to know. Then he'd ease back
Down, drop a single white digit between
His angled knees, mornings, afternoons, but
Especially evenings, when the gray
Line that separated that day
From cool memory grew long and uneven.

Our House

After breakfast, in dew jeweled grass
The first striped bee chases its soft buzz.

As we fasten black leather cleats tight,
The sun argues up beyond left field.

Bald headed dad dons his orange cup,
Slump-shouldered, drags a bag of scuffed balls

To the red dirt circle of mound, fits
A black brogan to the scarred white slab.

Forty-six feet away, I wait, a
Thirty inch wooden bat tapping red

Dust from the center of home plate that
I see, for the first time, is *our* house.

MY ELEVEN-YEAR-OLD

Wants me to be what I might have been.
So I have this short space to work in,
Where I can still be a hero, held up
By the air of memory and embellishment
On a pedestal of mound,
Tall and quiet, leaning in for a signal,
Slowly shaking it off, a rebel,
My cap pulled low, the bill bent just so,
Galvanizing the crowd,
An immortal enigma
Striking out the world.
My arm around his shoulders,
We leave the field
And the glow of the evening sun.
In a year he'll have
Figured out my stripes.

♦ ♦ ♦ ♦

YESTERDAY I CAME OUT OF A CLOUD

Before the sun could bend its bright face around the mountain,
The morning cereal sloshed and lent cool sugar, spoon-sized,
And I felt the freak that has me reach from inside, two-handed,
Fingertips flexing in on the lower ribs, like speedy cancer counting
The scattered days I have left under a Saturday of such suns.

As a child, I stomped across summers barefoot, smashed bees
With my baseball glove and memorized the kicks of certain pitchers—

Yesterday the gun shot a blank into the low sky over a textile town,
And I charged out from under the sound like a child running to first—
When my heart caught up with the hit of the first minute,
My face settled into the blank sky of the autumn foot race,
And I ran hard as the years would let me, up the smooth open road.

THE HIGH, DEEP OUTS

Fall down like human memory
Before a cold barrier of fence
That folds time back
Against a hero's effort—

You think that Papa
Had it right, the great fish
Bringing the old man
Just short
With great certainty—

We remember the slams
That barely clear
A leaping glove
And a forgiving wall;
We forget the high, deep outs,
The Series losers,
The thieves that died also
On their own crosses.

Beyond the Boxes of This Summer

There is the strong scent of something better
Beyond the dusty task of emptying boxes.

Last year's move left us forever in the on-deck circle,
Sifting through Seventeen years of life together,
Stuffed and stacked in brown grocery store boxes
Packed on one open side of this full basement,
Awaiting the Godot of that great and often-rumored yard sale,
Such a sweet domestic rapture that gets us through the slow months
When we will say so much for the Teenage Mutant
Ninja Turtles, the plastic Richard Petty race car,
The unicycles we never learned to ride,
Three old CPUs, old skis, and the hundred other
Sundry items that eluded the garbage can.

It is those mysterious artifacts that speak most
About our pace and style of living:
Boxes occupied by outdated bills,
Outgrown toys, tossed baseball cards
Suffering geometric contusions,
Certain oddities that even in their ambiguity
Insinuate more than my best work.

And yet there is a hint of change
In the tone of July that suggests
Truth will find us again beyond
All our sacred little history.
And we will bathe in it like Greek aristocrats,
So hopeful in what we've thrown away.

AT THE SCHOOL OF THE GAME WITH
LITTLE TOMMY WOLFE

Initially they tried him at first,
The boy so tall for his age,
But he stood there,
The girlish curls finally cut from his hair,
And gazed wistfully beyond the Southern mountains.
The next boy to play that bag
Found hearts and flowers, drawn in the dust.

From third he threw the ball tremendously
And anywhere he aimed but first.
He liked the view better and stayed
Till they moved him to left field.
It was a lovely place of wild clover
And occasional daffodils.
The action being rare out there,
He surveyed his territory
In a kind of awkward swagger,
Stopping once for a garter snake,
Then, holding his lanky arms out straight,
Pretended to be an eagle or a hawk.

At the plate he swung at every pitch,
Lunging and screaming with joy
At the infrequent connection.
But running the bases was his forte,
Every joint loose and moving—
So when he scored, in those brilliant
Million-footed moments, he knew
That life would never get better
Than running bases and the
Great gravity he felt between them.

Dr. Johnson Attends a Red Sox Opener

Carefully, he counts his steps up the runway,
Starting with his left foot, of course.
The crowd and its smells and hideous buzz,
He at first finds disconcerting, offensive, but
Then joins his own peculiar whistling
And wheezing and subvocalizations to its music,
To its primal harmony.

On the field this strange corruption of cricket
Moves swiftly; men dressed as prisoners
Run and slide and leap and wield a huge baton
With which they aim a great volley of cannon-like
Shots at the savages in the audience —
The "fielders" courageously protect the savages,
Who include nearly naked women, as unaware
Of their condition as Eve; men, stripped to the waist
And as well drawing no attention from the churched
Or the constables that guard the passages.

Dr. Johnson left Fenway, when they said it was over,
In his peculiar march, rolling his head and launching
The odd movements of his body that "motivated" him
As if independent of feet. Enough for him of hell,
This baseball, this queer century,
This backward, vermiculated country.

WHY BASEBALL WALTZES WITH LETTERS

A Faulkner sentence is an extra inning game,
Simply and finally playing through its
Will and exhaustion.

Third Base Coach signals are ee cummings poems—
Gimmicky, sure, but meaningful in their color
When you break the code.

The prisons play contests of Bukowski prose,
Where a stolen base may be a literal image
And everybody gambles nothing.

Weird killers load the bases at a
Stephen King Little League field, the sequel,
A grand slam promise at the bank.

Although Poe would never sit through nine,
His words are a dark season in the cellar,
A team leaving town and the death of a
Beautiful groupie.

Finally, Wolfe who wrote slugfest
Double-headers played to million-footed
Throngs, then flickered like so many other
Stars never meant for extra innings.

FIELD OF DREAMS—A LEGACY OF STRING

Down below the burgundy brick parsonage where we grew up,
By a dusty red dirt road
In the bad curve just before the old iron bridge
That shook with cars over Lyle Creek,
Despite my dad's best efforts as a citizen,
A trash dump grew in the best of Southern traditions:
Cans, papers, clothes, indistinguishable stinky messes
And masses—once even vats of industrial dye.

Venturing out on bikes in the kind of reconnaissance
That little kids with home-barbered crewcuts and
Red Kool-Aid smiles do, my brother Paul and I
Discovered, to our great delight, one summer day,
Several tremendous rolls of white string.

Paul was fascinated, and sat for hours,
Doubling and tripling the strands,
Tying them off every five or six feet for extra strength.
He had great patience,
And as he finished another and another length,
The lines began to appear in the side yard
Where we had neighborhood ball games.
First, there were baselines,
Running right to the fuzzy snowball bushes,
Left to cherry trees and the cow pasture fence.
Finally, after a glorious epiphany,
He stretched an extra thick cord
Around the outfield trees,
And "Katy bar the door," we had a fence
To argue about, a real-life measure of our clout.
And just so there would be no room for doubt,
Paul carefully measured each distance,
Nailing (which turned out to be unpopular)
The appropriate signage to the trees.

The games were savagely competitive:
Us, the neighbors and some kids from church—
We were pretty good, I suppose.
Through that summer and another one,
Paul's string fence hung tantalizingly.
And we watched our best rocket shots
Soar into the hundred year old limbs,
That as in life, despite our best efforts,
Decided which side of the fence
The ball would fall on.

◆ ◆ ◆ ◆

HE'S THE CHILD

That can't quite tell his father what he wants,
So he learns to shuffle his way out to right field,
Learns to study the three varieties of pine trees
Behind the outfield fence, the creek below
As it bubbles over smooth rocks into a culvert,
And he identifies with the redirected water,
Holds his spot in the lineup like a dammed river—
At the plate he's the child that walks or strikes out,
Waits it out like a careful-eyed warrior, but
Inside, his mind stops, and he floats across
The bleachers, beyond the bright concession stand
And hovers till his heart tells him clearly,
To run or walk away.

There Was a Ball Game Somewhere

Before video parlors, PCs and
Nintendo, on our ragged bicycles
We scrambled to one house or the other—
Hefners, Peelers, then the Swansons who moved
In the neighborhood, sometimes the Coffeys
From church, or the Swansons' friends from their church—
For the really big affairs with full teams,
Baseball games with football scores. Out in the heat
Most of the day, just breaking for lunchtime—
Easy pitches and little guys taking
Big cuts, ghost runners and no catcher, weird
Rules like groundrule doubles for balls driven
Into the short cow pasture fence in left
Or how to play a pop fly that rolled off
The eight-sided parsonage roof or smacked
The huge oak trees in center field or the
Maple in right-center.

Barefoot sometimes, always in shorts only,
Crew cuts and popsicle stains on our mouths—
Before Play Station and VCRs there
Was a baseball game somewhere in dust and
Sweltering heat, a game to be played by
Our rules only.

EXTERNAL LOCUS OF CONTROL

Luckless Lonnie played third
On an undefeated Little League team
Where he complained
With great impunity—
Every ball took a bad hop,
Every throw slipped,
Every runner was out to get him,
Even our own guys
In practice.

Solid built and lefty,
At the plate he served
A separate volley of sad laments.
When his full swing struck emptily,
He twisted into the dirt,
Or wasn't set,
Or lost the dirty ball in the sun,
Or slung the bat
Because of the cheap batting glove,
Then moaned back to the dugout
To take an uncomfortable seat
In my memory.

I imagine Lonnie now,
Somewhere in the continental U.S.,
On permanent disability,
Tremendously overweight
In a chair that rocks,
Swivels, and reclines
But doesn't work right,
Sipping on a drink
That has too much ice in it,
Watching a TV show that sucks, and
Thinking about the good ole days.

MIDWEST CITY, 1970

I was the youngest,
So when dad looked at me,
Through 102° of Oklahoma heat,
And felt the sting of my sarcasm
As I pounded the choking dust
On that playground plate,
He mumbled back at my brothers,
Fifteen yards beyond in the
Dead grass of the outfield either way,
"Why is the bad hop
Always the last one?"

Batting practice, morning,
Vacation visiting my Air Forced brother,
Interned at Tinker Base but
Forever in the shadow of Nam.
The heat was not the Carolina
Swelter we were used to.
It was oven baking—
Magnifying glass on insects.
But we all needed the swings
And the tosses and the catches
And the river of sweat that
Sapped my legs rubbery at thirteen,
Thirteen and full of so much
Big talk that meant nothing
More than dust rising in heat
And one more swing
For an imaginary fence.

BIG BLUE

Was the first guy
To really learn to cuss good.

He went to the office
About once a week for cussing in Algebra.
The sweet old lady teacher always
Said the same thing, her wire-rimmed glasses
Swinging on a cord at her wrinkled neck,
"I'm simply mortified!" as she shooed him
Out into the hallway
As if he were part of an unworkable equation.

Big Blue was skinny and small-boned,
But he nailed line drives at the ball games,
Had the arm for third,
And he was creepy tough
With an aura of craziness about him—
Who would fight the dude anyway!—
His cleats up sliding,
A possum's equivocal grin.

Big Blue could take a beaning
Like a mosquito bite—
Could rattle the opposing pitcher
With matter-of-fact death threats,
Left the rest to reputation.

Blue kept dark, ugly bruises all down his legs,
And scars he could never explain.

WATCHING KEENER WARM UP

When you're twelve or thirteen,
There's a dread you get
Watching a dangerous pitcher warm up,
That is like nothing else in sports.

You can watch the other basketball team
Shuffling through lay-ups, gliding high
And smooth, and you may get a sense
Of gloom.
They will rebound over you, steal
The ball from you, but they will not
Send death or blindness toward your head.

In football
That lineman may pulverize you, trample you,
Shove you into the next county, but the fear
Is not the same.

Watching Keener warm up, a six-foot
Twelve-year-old with a teenager's
Nasty disposition, a jerky delivery
And a curve that started toward your noggin,
Brought bile to your mouth, and a
War of butterflies in your stomach,
Like looking off the edge of something
Knowing it's the only way down.

MOOSE WAS A FREE SPIRIT

Had a mop of sun bleached hair
In the dubious year of our Lord, 1970.
The adults around here called him a Beatle.

Moose was a free spirit—
You could tell by the way he ran the bases,
His hair flying behind him from under his cap,
The same when he charged after
A fly ball in center field,
Diving head-on into a knot of outfield grass,
Coming up, undaunted and throwing hard.

The girls liked Moose;
He was not afraid of them like most of us—

Moose was a free spirit.
When he dove into shallow water at the lake
And broke his neck that summer,
The news traveled like electricity—
And jolted us for a while—
Till we went on, immortally,
Because we were only eighth graders,
Immune to gravity
And the ever-growing odds against us.

JIM BURNS

Had the kind of deafness an ump must have.
A pleasant heavyset middle-aged man,
I think he drove a Sundrop truck by day;
Warm evenings he sweated behind the plate,
Moisture darkening his dark blue shirt.
From behind the backstop we heckled him,
Eight-year-old boys attacking
With bold intensity, inventing names
That strung together a chain of insults.
Jim the Butter-Blubber-Blob Burns, we called,
Whether strike or ball, cheering for no one.

We were nice when we talked to him between
Innings, when he stood by the fence waiting
For the warm-ups, but then he bent over
Home and dusted red sand from white rubber
And the barrage began in earnest: Jim
The Blind, Bald, Bow-Legged Burns. We could have
Been birds perched on a power line beyond
The outfield fence, because Jim never re-
acted, just bellowed his version of the
Strike zone, so good at it, he's the only
Ump I remember.

BACK AT YOUR OLD SCHOOL

Twenty-five years later
Cows still graze serenely within sight
Of the ball field and the hard paved track—
But the lots are asphalted and the kids
Lease sports cars and pickups
That squeal tires as you and your
Oldest son stretch beside what was once
The baseball diamond, now brick buildings
Grown out over foul territory.
But every now and then,
When you look up quickly,
You see a struck-out ghost or two
And a translucent pitcher waiting
Patiently for the field to right itself,
For a batter to brave the years,
For the spring wind that cuts
Across the knoll where
Your old school squats outside of time.

He May as Well Have Been Struck by a Car

The way that God zapped the boy as he
Swung his arm forward behind a high kick
Was as if something heavy, powerful
Had delivered an invisible lick
And his limp arm looped the ball in a dull
Arc toward an open-mouthed batter,
Who watched the dead ball dribble to a stop.
Nothing moved on the diamond—no chatter
From the infield, no buzz in the bleachers
While the Little League pitcher crossed his arms
Over his belly and turned slow circles
Out in front of the mound like an insect
Stricken by poison—till his older
Brother leaped the dugout fence to hug him
And the other kids observed the slow dance
Of the seizures that would sweep that boy
Right out of the game like the ice cold glare
Of the car's high beams, about to crush the
Lanky redheaded child they called Troy.

THE BALL WAS DIRTY

With deep brown scuffs across
The wide crescent sections,
Like a badly scarred face.

The field was sandy, red clay
Packed hard and salted with
Bits of mica and broken glass.

The children wore second-hand clothes—
Pants too short; sleeves rolled up
Over scabby elbows; scabs, too, on

The lower legs that showed
Above dark blue socks, collapsing
From broken elastic around

Bony, purple ankles, blackened
By a long summer's soil—the red smirch
Of Kool-Aid smiles revealed cavities,

Some of the boys big-eared
And slouchy, others nearly full-grown
With raw good looks.

The catcher had a mitt and a mask,
Dark bruises on chalky white legs—
He wore shorts and squatted

Deep in the hot dust—the pitcher
Was cock-eyed and kicked
Toward third base where the

Third baseman and shortstop
Were left-handed forcing right
Hander gloves—they had no coach

And they wanted to fight
Instead of finish the game.
How we beat them,
I'll never know—or how we left
With teeth and not enough sense to be scared.

THE LITTLE GUYS

From Little League, the little guys
Are the ones that I remember.
Sure, there was the twelve-year-old
Six-footer that left-handed a homer
Three hundred feet to the red dirt bank
By the gravel parking lot,
And there were the three or four
Big guys that bleached us like sheets
With corkscrew windups and slingshot missiles;
Dad took me to the x-ray room one night,
But I was not a little guy like Jessup or Coffey
Or Hatley or the young Bailey or the young Whitener.
These fellows dug in every time,
Hard-faced young-uns with 60s boy crewcuts
Or flattops like Johnny U.
They played second base and shortstop
And even catcher—
They were the little guys, weighing half
What the home run hitters like Reed and Hefner
And Walker and the older Bailey weighed.
They batted leadoff and drew walks and
Hit triples into the right-field corner with
The game on the line.
These sub–five footers owned the base paths,
Sold their guts in strawberry slides
That toughened their already toughened hides.
The little guys snatched the game from
The big boys, I believe, as memory
Is my servant.

YOU THINK OF ALL THE TIME

Spent sitting on the sidelines of a ball field
As the pollen stuffed the air with sneezes,
And you connected so gently
In the molasses of crisp spring evenings
With the fatal issues on the base paths,
When to score or to be out
Sent a quiver through your knees,
And you could barely look
As your prodigy stepped in with two strikes,
A hopeful runner at third,
The outcome of the game teetering
On this next charged moment;
You did, in fact, close your itchy eyes,
And the ping of the metal bat,
The quick harmony of mother
And father voices shouting, cheering,
Are what you miss—
Seven years after he put the game
Out of his life,
You imagine that dusty, red-headed boy
Sprinting for first, his narrow shoulders
Pushing hard and forward,
His hands grabbing great swatches of air
And slinging them behind him.

EASTER AFTERNOON UNSPLINTERED

Between network round ballers, grocery store,
A windy run through the bright green forest,

Kids outgrown colored eggs, baskets, bunnies,
Now clicked on to Nintendo Major League—

Yet, a slow hour
Before twilight we toss a baseball and
Bat it lightly toward the grassy field
Overgrown with purple flowers, fragrant
When you bend down to search an errant
Hit or a lost throw, its beauty raw as the
Mountain, heavy in its four shades of
Evening green behind my twelve-year-old.
A father and two sons, we play together
In a warm resurrection of sunshine;
We connect with line drives of the heart.
So beyond the tomb of busy separation,
I watch the thin profile of my sixteen-
Year-old lope under a soft fly ball, his
Shadow barely a shadow, his long idle
Glove closing perfectly.

JEFF WHO SAID

"If you are young, gather old bricks,"
Lived in an apartment building
Behind Wrigley Field—
You know, where they used to sit
On rooftops to watch
The endless slate of day games.

Jeff was the first real poet
I knew—in fact, went to high school
And college with. He was amiable
But aloof when confronted—
And left these here hills,
Left a local theatre production
Of *Grease* halfway through its run.

His daring lack of responsibility
Took his poetry to a new level
For me, and I studied the words,
Undid the bow of the lines
To see how he worked his rhymes,
And I looked for him, always
In a lawn chair, atop a nameless
Stack of habitations, his dark blue Cubs hat
Pulled low, a thin feminine hand grasping a glass
Of Scotch he couldn't afford.

Jeff left, but I stayed—
And through the graceless years
I've primed his art, and
Gathered up old bricks
That smash my heart.

PASS THE PETER PAN

When I was a college freshman,
I met this huge guy from SC
Who was the coolest hippie
I'd ever seen.
He had the act down pat and
I wanted to be just like him—
Went to hard rock concerts with him,
Swayed with the little girls
In the old hippie dances
Down front of the stage;
While every new guitarist
Donned a garage jump suit,
Trying to look like Clapton
We wore ragged jeans
Embroidered with colorful patches
And faded black t-shirts
With a pocket at the breast—
We were the coolest hippies
That anyone had ever seen.

When spring came
And I suggested a baseball game,
He sneered—
And I explained, using all the
Mandatory "likes" and "mans,"
The awkward green beauty of the game,
A beauty that defies ordinary meaning.
He sneered.
I sensed I had reached
The length of my chain.
"Baseball is as common
As peanut butter,"
He hissed—
And I strained at my collar,
Strained till my throat ached
And my eyes burned.

DH

David Henry prayed for me,
Prayed for good enough grades
To play spring baseball—

My freshman roommate
At a junior college in the mountains,
He'd watched the fall season
From academic probation
On an angry hillside
Where he drank beer
And smoked cigarettes
And thought up prayers for me.

David was short, wiry,
Had big brown eyes, nose,
And thick wavy brown hair—
He looked Jewish,
But he talked Charlotte, NC,
And man did he want
To play shortstop—

David Henry prayed for me
Along with some flute playing
Hippie from California that
Swore he knew Jackson Browne;
They swayed in the dorm room floor
Like holy cobras
And prayed for my soul
In tongues, sweet and alien.

But I went on living
Like the devil anyway,
And the spring came
Without David's good grades.
He watched again from
High up on a hillside—
Smoked a little more
And finally gave up
On my soul
Just before I transferred
And took it with me.

SPARKY

A best friend from my college years,
He hated most of the sports
Except for the college football games
Where he conveyed a pint of gin
In a cowboy boot, by halftime
Passing a joint in a student crowd
Next to the Boy Scout troops.
(He claimed to have been an Eagle himself
And confided this to the alarmed Scout Master,
Who was little afraid of this wild-eyed hippie
That cursed as easily as an angry coach.)

Wiry, blonde and mop-haired,
Sparky holed up in his room
While we followed the Braves
On those first years of cable,
Days of Niekro, knuckleballs, and losing ugly.
But it was consistent entertainment
And we converted Sparky over to the faith
Halfway through the summer,
He knew the players
And caught on to some of the subtleties
Of the game.
Sparky was a genius
In his area of science and soon
Began to understand the game as a kind
Of uncontrolled experiment,
Not unlike his own life—which rambled
Wilder and wilder with days and days
Of white lines on mirrors, then
The beer and Quaaludes during the
Ball games to calm him before
A mad run through the downtown bars.
I watched him pass out on a half-stuffed,
Faded beanbag chair, after talking back
To Carson and then Snyder, his wire-rimmed
Glasses bent from some anonymous punch.

One game night he concluded that
The Braves could never win big
With Niekro as their ace: If success comes
Proportionately with the amount of control
You can exert over the continuous series
Of outcomes, then you must know
Where the ball is going.
(I remember agreeing but thinking
About Niekro's success in '69.)

When I pointed out to Sparky
That the act of following the games
Was in a sense an exertion
Of self-control, he stopped.

About the time Niekro retired
His knuckleball in Cleveland,
Sparky, our own Mr. Knuckle Ball,
Died in a drunken, early
Morning accident—
Going out with a flutter
Instead of a bang.

A Sunday Afternoon

I'd done my long run—
On the luxurious, damp carriage trails
Between Bass Lake and the manor
At Moses Cone Park—
Rode on up the orange-yellow mountain
To an Education Conference,
Grabbed my buddy Kevin from Kinston,
Said let's go grab Brad and grub
And watch the playoffs somewhere.

So we sat first on the back veranda in rockers,
Then upstairs in Brad's brown rectangular house—
A well-built two stories of cracker box in Foscoe, NC—
   Waiting for the game to end
   To go eat;
Sipping the house beer,
Talking the academic jargon
That low-level academics aspire to,
Discussing the cause and effect of illiteracy,
   Waiting for the game to end
   To go eat;
Sipping another and another
Of the guest beer
That Brad broke out for the occasion,
Finally retreating to the basement,
The big TV, the stereo—
The most eclectic wall of sound
Ever built for a temporary evening of
   Waiting for the game to end
   To go eat—
While the Braves and Mets played on
And on in pouring rain
Like something too crazy
For even a Kinsella story—
So we sipped another

And thought about the particular
Images it might take for
A study of cultural illiteracy—
Lou Reed and Joe Frank and
Van Morrison and more Joe Frank
As the weirdness grew
Like a fungus,
Like an addiction,
Like the game—
And Brad became more
Prufrock than Brad,
And still the rain fell
Like an existentialist horror
Where everyone is up against the wall
Of sound and extra innings,
    Waiting for the game to end
    To go eat.

Later, over pizza,
Kevin, who'd had a heart attack at 29,
Confided that dying's
Not so bad as you think.

I'd Rather Be There

Scared half to death I was going to bean
The next guy or the one after, days of
Wet dark green grass that smelled like life—and yet
I did not know it at the time, in fact,
Took this trick of memory to get in-
side my own nose and sniff the spring rain mov-
ing in the flat gray clouds above, to feel
My leg kicking like a compass needle
In its cool circle, petty gravity
Holding the right cleat in its deep pivot—

I'd rather be there on a warm April
Saturday than in this stifling chapel
Respiring stiff funeral flowers and
The ambrosial charge of perfume and
Cheap cologne. White pews and walls and choir robes
And cross and ceiling and casket—all more
An absence of life. And the hammer of
The minister in the headache coil of
Amplification, simplification
That garrotes the living—"O Lost!"
I can not think myself back again.

RAYMOND'S TIME

When he was young,
Raymond was wiry in a way that
Defined the word—
Lean, strong, agile, a second-sacker
With radar for the shots that come that way,
A malleable wit and nature
Easily bent to rib or take ribbing
Later, a gamer on the church softball
And volleyball teams—
The hardest worker I'd ever seen,
Two jobs and cutting firewood
For a world that suddenly begged for it.

But for me Easters were Raymond's time.
At the sunrise service,
Half-disabled by the lack of sleep,
We were mesmerized each year
When he sang "Were You There?"
And his voice trembled
Like the very body of Jesus
Dragging the cross to Calvary,
And a sorrow and beauty
Almost palpable filled the church,
As the morning light streamed
Through the stained glass windows
In that cathartic moment
When Raymond became one with his Lord.

ELLIS HAD A STEEL PLATE IN HIS HEAD

And pins in a leg forever stiff;
He had so little feeling in his hands
He caught and fielded the ball barehanded.

On the grassy field beside the scout hut
He was a pitching machine—
Overhand or underhand, for both teams,
Before our meetings and after them
In the summer.
It was an all-arm delivery,
And sometimes a come-backer
Smacked him on the shin;
But he would just reach down and
Pick up the ball as if pain
Were not a part of his world.

Bald, middle-aged and solid built,
Ellis was the closest thing we
Ever had to those new robot pitchers.
But Ellis cared where the ball went,
And he put his pipe down,
Forgot his Taxi, the war wound,
The bad wreck, a life of hard labor
And always a second job;
Ellis pitched for both sides
Till the sun went down
And the game was over.

A True Story

Barney lived near Startown Crossroads
And often could be seen
At the store, or standing in the intersection,
Waving or shouting at people he seemed to know.
A thin, lean-faced man, ruddy cheeked
From years outside, a day or two's worth
Of gray stubble peppered on his chin,
Barney wore overalls, sometimes a red cap
As he swept the tile-floored store,
The slanted asphalt parking lot.
But this is a true story, and Barney
Not some metaphor from *The Last Picture Show*,
Nor was he some ex–major league slugger
Doomed to oblivion by a protagonist's beanball.
Just a very simple man marking his time
On the planet with a broom,
Wagging a finger at the increasing blur of traffic
That finally got him at sixty-two,
Dead center and true,
His arms reaching into the air.

IN '69

Twelve and persistent
As the worst salesman
That ever stuck a toe in a door,
I began telling people at the church
That we were going to see the Braves.

Now the interstate to Atlanta was still
A long, strung-out thing back then,
But I told my buddy Coffey and the Hefners
And some of the men who stood out front
In ties and shirtsleeves,
Smoking by the wall before the service.
And soon it become known
That we were gong on an autumn Sunday,
With my frugal Dad, the dedicated minister,
Carefully picking a Lutheran church to attend—
More carefully than our field-level seats,
First base side, overweight Ken Johnson pitching
For the Cubs, the lanky Ron Reed for the Braves
In a bright afternoon of contrasts.

My head wheeled from side to side
In the round stadium, trying to take it
All in—the sheltered preacher's son,
A bit scared of all the beer drinkers,
Amazed at the wildness and color of it all,
The remarkable green open space of the field.
Then I turned away for a blink,
I missed the sudden pop of the ball as it left Aaron's bat,
Crashing in blue seats above
Chief Noc-A-Homa's tent.
I willed the trip, the game, the day,
Then blinked at a bright piece of history
In '69.

AFTER GRADUATION, DARKNESS

Is the unsealed envelope
We fold twice and fall into.

Waiting, waiting for the game
To come home from its commercials.

We are somewhere beyond darkness
Where a chip sends us and an actor

Hollers his endless lawnmower lines
Across the width of a screen

We thought too big for this,
Just right for our Cy Young heroes.

After graduation, darkness
Seeps into the valley of the Jacob Fork.

We dim the living room lamps and feel
A river of it pouring across the front yard
Out toward the mountains
Where quietness ages slowly.

THERE IS NOTHING, IN SPORT, LIKE
A NEW BASEBALL

Without seeing one, I can feel it in
My hand, fresh from an umpire's dark blue
Canvas bag: a sweet white sphere—but not as
Smooth as one might think a palomino's
Forgiving hide.

It feels a bit like your dry face after
A very close shave, and the odor is
Quite like a new leather belt or wallet—
A good pitcher could smell the sharp break in
The face of the rock—and every baseball
Has one: a mouth, closed eyelids, a low brow,
The receding hairline of red stitches.

In sport what can you compare with this orb?
A puck? A grainy leather basketball?
Without seeing one, I can feel how it
Rests in the open palm of my right hand,
The excitement of placing two fingers
With or against the lightly rising seams,
Rubbing it with my glove propped between my
Elbow and hip while a batter fidgets
Inside a perfectly fresh line of chalk.

A WORLD SO SIMPLE

That your biggest problem
Is deciding how you'll hold the ball—
With or across the seams.
And some say turn it this,
Others turn it that way—
So sure of this little knowledge
They show you where
The blisters should burst
On your "gone soft" hands.

A world so simple
You can hold the whole thing
In either hand.

♦ ♦ ♦ ♦

BB TEAMS

Are really just companies these days. See
Their news on CNBC, not ESPN;
Watch them merge players, little companies
Into the latest portfolio of investment;
Blow a wish across a GM's wisdom;
And when a season's over, or before,
Divest, divest, spin off and reverse split.

Is there somebody in there somewhere—hey,
Can you hear me?

DOCK IN THE COUNTRY OF TRAGEDY

Radical enough
To fetch the calculated gaze of a cool white poet,
An academic, bearded, pedigreed
And anxious to lay out that
Liberal and "objective" simpatico,
To provide an insider's studied argument
As to the sociological whys and wherefores
Regarding this impecunious, misunderstood underdog.

But, Dock, you were just another
Man, eluding your own potential in favor of rage,
Hawking charisma and unfocused guts.
A no-hitter on acid?
Give me a break—
Or something more tangible
Than the assurance of memory.
I loved to watch you, Dock:
Smooth, fast, nearly bold as Gibson.
From dynamo to domino, finally
Waiting for the tumble.

HRABOSKY

Oh, we loved to watch Al;
He was mad like us,
Or like we thought we were.
He was power and passion
And self-parody rolled into
One stocky body—
It was wrestling or relief pitching;
There could have been nothing else,
Just as there was only one pitch
And one way he could meet with himself
Behind the mound
While the batter clicked clods from cleats
And the runners fidgeted
Toward whatever stake of territory
They dared against the madness.

When he hurled 360 to face the plate—
The dark eyes, the hair, the handlebar—
Looked more like an executioner
Than anything we'd seen since Gibson.
We loved to watch Al;
He was mad just like we wanted to be.

CURT

You had that flood of words,
An intellect beyond typical ballplayer brains,
And the abdominal workings to challenge the beast.

So the fist that would squeeze you
Till your face turned the split purple of the hanged man
Could only grip and slip—for you had become
The unopenable bottle,
Your untouchable independence corked within.

For the prolonged boring committee hearings
You had that flood of words and the proud tone
And the singular notion
That this was about way more than you
Or money or privilege—

When I saw you on Roy Firestone
A year or two before your death,
You talked like a retired professor,
Not a defunct ballplayer; and I could tell then
As sure as every player is overpaid, now, that
You had won
Whatever it was, Curt.

THE SHORTSTOP SEES A WILDCAT

In the grim gray city
Where the clouds ride the river in,
Where Canada squats
Beyond a brand new tunnel,
A city of smoke and labor
Resurrected from the South.

Socks pulled tight in cleats that claw
For safety and flesh through flannel,
The hardest face this side
Of a spear or whip,
While electricity stitches
A cut in the summer sky,
The missile of Cobb
Breaks from the fog
And the shortstop has that unearthly
Feeling you get in the mountains
When you hear that primal yowl.

THERE IS A CERTAIN SOPHISTICATION

In blundering well and often—
The words, the meanings, the ideas,
An art maybe, that has to be nurtured,
Practiced, perfected.

I see an old man,
Good for a one-liner commercial,
Relaxed in a casual interview
On a cable sports show,
A face that sags a bit
In that familiar hound dog mien,
A body still stocky under
Shoulders mildly stooped.
The calmness is still there,
The calmness to handle
Some of the greatest pitchers
To ever toe the rubber,
The confidence to jolt
Fifteen homers in World Series games,
And that certain sophistication
That lets you know
He's no average Berra.

GEHRIG'S NUMBERS

Thanks to our need to qualify everything
At the end of this millennium—
Because we are the ones here who can—
Lou Gehrig gets rated number 34
Among the top fifty athletes of the century
By the all-knowing sport wizards at ESPN.

My kids watch and learn
As the clip rolls and the numbers are read
Along with the rare b & w footage—
This everyday guy who swung
In the Bambino's shadow
And averaged 150 RBIs for eleven years
(Imagine that happening today,
The god-commercial worship we'd be
Bloodied with)—
Even my cynical fifteen-year-old
Was shocked by the sheer
Heft of that figure, that
Mountain of production.
And I'm sorry, birdies,
But Ripken couldn't hold
The shadow of this man's jockstrap.

◆ ◆ ◆ ◆

THE GRAVITY OF MEMORY

You knew just where he was going
When you saw him press the tips of his fingers
Together as in a prayer or a childhood
Game; you knew he'd gone far away from the
Clatter of cleats on the cement dugout floor.
He wore long gray sideburns then, well after
The glory days; he wore one ring, the '69.
Sometimes, in a close game, you'd see him pull it
Off, slide it on the other way, his chin resting
In his palm, elbow propped against his knee,
Only the gravity of memory
Keeping him in this world.

THE END OF THE CENTURY

And the comparisons are inevitable—
All us fanatics must know for sure:
Who is the greatest athlete
Of the last hundred years?

It will come down to the final two
As ESPN is nice enough to decide for us.
And why not? When we are so frantic
To be told, gripping the sweaty cans
Of our beer, adjusting the angle
Of our recliners—we are a fallen race
Of men who have managed to catch
Ourselves just like this, in the action
Of watching action.

A week will turtle by in the office break rooms
And out by the furniture loading dock
And in the student lounge, even.
Michael or the Babe, what do ya' think?
Black or white, yin or yang?

And I will be called stupid, racist, out of touch
For taking the Babe—though I love the other
Game for the way it turns anger into dunks,
Revenge into blocks, violence into good defense—
The way it brings hope to the hopeless and money, too.

So the week will drift along while I defend the Bambino
Against my family of sports fans, point to the support
Of his numbers, the sheer ineffable dominance of peers,
The pitching record, and the stolen bases. I point to
These things as if to a pie chart, but Michael will get it,
Here at his high-flying end of the century;
And nobody, not a single arguing one of us
Will listen to Satchel Paige, who cocked his cap
To the side and said, "Don't look back."

ANOTHER STRANGE NIGHT IN
THE MONTH OF REGGIE

House-settling messages tap through the floor,
And I tug at my worn-out Dockers like a third base coach
As I sit out the silence of Texan bats again,
All those beautiful Latino hammers forgotten
How to drive nails, when Reggie could if only
The years would take him back—

Surf out
To pop music charity concert: bright flashy lights,
Smoke and rock stars that measure love by the inch.
I rub my thumb across the faint stubble of evening beard
And think about Ezra Pound—scared of American
Communists, Supreme Court protection for the NAACP—
When Donald Hall interviewed him in the early 60s,
The description of his uncertain triangle face—
Then Jimmy Page playing "Whole Lotta Love"
For Kosovar refugees—
Then David Bowie with a stretched smooth face
And a River Phoenix haircut, crooning, "Rebel, Rebel—"

Surf back
To Texan silence, Clemens rocking in a Cy Young groove,
Still no Reggie to ride the cavalry in till the earth shakes
Under horses;
Instead, Reggie dickering somewhere over a muscle car,
Horsepower, and duking it out with Charles Barkley
For angry black athlete of the century.
I saw Reggie lose once on Jeopardy, with a dull
Unanswering smirk that said, like Saturn, Baby,
I still got my rings.

FROM THE DAYS OF HARD AND HARDER

Gibson shot a spike into the moon over St. Louis.
It was within reach when he stood the mound,
Besides Russell, Mays, and Ali, the supreme athlete
Of a golden decade of supreme athletes.

Gibson sent a shiver all the way across the river,
All-American corn fed white boys dug in
A bit troubled if they'd been there
In the glare of the stare and seen the huge hand
Hide the white flash of baseball just long enough
So it appeared as if from under a shell in the mitt,
Or worse into your ribs till you doubled over
Like a cowboy struck in a saloon; but his was
A mound you didn't charge,
Where he did more for civil rights
Than ten thousand marchers,
Though there was nothing passive
In his resistance.
Gibson shot a spike into the moon
Over St. Louis, you better believe it!

Longest Names for Back-to-Back Homers— A Found Poem

To end up on the same team
Might seem improbable,
This Stankiewicz and Grudzielanek.
After all, this is the American pastime,
Home of Smiths, Williamses, and Jacksons.

What was Felipe thinking, that silly Dominican,
When he made that card on a hot August night in '97?
Did he check the spellings, glancing back
Several times at the computerized roster?
Did he dream those long balls
In his managerial prescience?
Knowing the twenty-three letters
Of their consummate names
Would whip that Dallessandro and Nicholson,
That Yastrzemski and Conigliaro,
That Petrocelli and Yastrzemski,
And just too bad, too bad
For the many with 20.

Bermuda High Days

We are stalled like one of those
Bermuda highs that sits on the South
And holds it down in August.
The Braves are in a tailspin
For the first time in years,
And we are stalled, unable to
Complete the chores that
Have chosen us, that the gods
Have given us; our karma
Is stuck in the bottle, not good,
Or the bad it could be, and
The Braves are plunging beyond
The horizon of wins.
There are these things
Which wait for us to do,
For the right time, the right temperature,
But we are stalled and waiting,
Waiting for the first bright
Windy day.

◆ ◆ ◆ ◆

Your 95 mph Fastball Won't Get You in the Draft Anymore

Like a 1400 on your SAT won't get you into Harvard
And American Express will continually turn you down
Because your salary goes up slower than their expectations.

Who will get through the traffic jam?
Who will grow the nerves to win the new game?
Who will sop up the spoils, raise a toast in the ruins?

Let me write one tremendously long line like the horizontal bar at
    the high jump pit—
See how I fail, even at this?
But my failure is merely a failure of margins,
And your 95 MPH fastball is nothing more than a metaphor
These days.

OVERCAST SUNDAY

While rain taps against the roof,
The cat scratches his naked complaint
On the door leading down to his basement.
Like tending a baby, I consider his checklist
And leave the flurry of Red Sox runners
In this mad playoff game at Fenway.
I leave rabid fans to hold hopes, fright, and
"Reverse the Curse" signs, for a mongrel cat
Named Skeeter, who day after day offers to me
His unconditional indifference—
And the royalty of his mouse killing presence—
Far more than the whiny fans of Fenway
And their funny Boston talk
Or the effervescent ghosts of games lost
On overcast Sunday afternoons.

THE DAY YOU LOOK FOR BRIGHT THINGS

Like memories that keep you moving
Up the steep path at the bottom of Baker's Mountain—
A day of cobwebs you clear as the trail narrows
Between muscadine vines and fallen limbs—
In your head you do the same, clear the debris
That builds in September, that bursts in October
In the hardwood leaves that panel this eastern side
Which slopes lazily in against itself.

The bright memories help you climb across cracked rocks,
Fissured into curves that slash back south through red leaves,
Glistening like a third glass of wine on a quiet afternoon,
Memories of classic baseball,
Of the excited voices that brought it into cool autumns,
Gowdy calling Gibson and Lonborg—
While young men zipped in body bags
Were sent home just in time for the Series,
Red and yellow memories
Of when you were ten
And it all seemed to make some scary sense,
Like your baldheaded dad who kept his confidence
In the pulpit in 1967.

The bright memories chase you **now**
All the way to the top of the little hogback
Where the stack of satellites
Holds you in the dancing cadmium sunlight,
In these blessed last days of the nineties.

MY FOOT IS ON THE PEDAL

And the nights whisper secrets.
The dark October interval of precocious scarlet sunsets
Leads this rambler by the hand
To ponder the gray teeth marks of winter
Beyond what heroes October clenches
In the stainless teeth of its pure future.

My foot is on the pedal
And the Red Sox are winning—
Leaves, cadmium and blood red,
Dance in New England breezes;
Donald Hall shuffles across a Southern stage,
Sets the horrible edge of his grief
In hearts opened through esurient ears.

My foot is on the pedal and
My oldest child waits for me
On a bus beyond midnight;
Time clowns its slow way
On a Saturday like an old man
Shuffling across the stage. The Braves lost
And Belle beat the Sox, I will
Tell him.
Tired though he is, shaking his
Red hair back, he will ask,
What about the Mets?

A NIGHT

Of shagging flies
Under the full moon,
And you a dark silhouette
Against the darker silhouette
Of the mountain, which
Steadies itself
In the August heat
While you jog toward
The smaller orb made
Of sad, slow animal,
Plant and tree—
And notice the sudden
Scatter of tiny rabbits
In the freshly mown field
Beyond the backyard.
Your son's metal bat pings—
The lab chases the rabbits
To the length of his fence
And barks, himself sad
And fierce.

Another night
In the South at
The dead end of summer,
You are barefoot
In dry, crunchy grass—
No wind to cry Mary,
Just a high sky
Slick with starry fortunes.

You and your son
Play on silently
As the floodlights
From the house follow
Your melancholy pace—
As if this were some
Terrible defeat or
Grave tragedy
Instead of just a night
Of shagging flies
Under the full moon.

THIS IS THE DAY

When every relationship and previously
Understood concept feels tenuous.
Albeit the gravity grows weak
And the voices that rise
Are not the sanguine few
You remember as wise, the coaches
That actually "knew" something
Beyond the roar of their anger—

Now your days on the field
Are gone or have slipped
Into the churn and become
Sweet buttered memories,
Not the indecisive hell
Of rounding second not knowing
Where the ball was and the
Third base coach hollering
At a player on the bench
While they trapped you in
A rundown.

You recall
The running outfield catches
Of a sunny childhood, not the
Dark liner lost in the lights till
It roared toward you
Like a car with one headlight.

Memory is the shaky tightrope
You wrap your dreams around;
And faith in the past, the balance
To get you through this day.

THIS FLAMING AFTERNOON

I box my way through the heat,
Into the woods, up the washed-out hills,
Across the scraped-up tree roots that reach in mud and sand,
Over the muck of two creek beds,
Within the range of horse flies,
Their uncanny chase and midair bites.

I feel the hot itch of my sweaty flesh,
Stretch for the unreachable red splotches.
The burn in my legs rages as I push
The first two miles, then turn back
With the wind, wobbling back up the Church Road
To the house, thinking of third base seats
At tonight's Crawdad game, clinging
To a strip of grass as the traffic shoots by
Both ways—rumbling pickup trucks,
SUVs of all persuasions and trendy colors.
A blue poodle makes a run at my ankles,
Then stops short, pain and confusion
In its lean look.
I attack the hill in a ragged gait, 90 degrees;
A carload of teenagers scream at me,
Four feet from my ear, 55 miles per hour.
I picture the perfect green diamond,
Imagine the soft cushion I will carry
To the cement bleachers,
And I finish my flight toward solitude.

Sometimes You Have to Come In

Last night I watched Hernandez, the Devil Ray reliever,
Dispatch a pitch into Brian Hunter's jaw, 96 mph.
The replay was nauseating, but Hunter walked
Steadily back to the dugout, like away from a wreck.

That afternoon I'd watched Sport South,
A show that chronicled baseball fights,
And that worst one of all, of course the finale, in '65
When Marichal leveled Roseboro
With the chop of his bat, and punches flew till police arrived.

Some fingers pointed at Koufax,
Who refused to throw at Marichal, or anybody,
It would seem, so Roseboro rifled
His return tosses, buzzing Marichal's head, instead.

I thought of myself so long ago
Contemplating a stray fastball
As it zoomed toward the batter's ribs,
Shouting, too late, Duck!

The sickest part of the game for me,
It ravaged my own breath,
Walloped my heart for a minute,
Until like lucky Hunter,
He took his place
On the steady legs God gave him.
And I repented, selfishly sought redemption,
Although I knew I *had* to pitch.

HOW MANY NIGHTS

Just like this,
A different man with the same dark eyes,
Measuring you through cigarette smoke
Over the rim of a drink glass,
As the bartender clinks the empties
On to a tray bound for the kitchen
And the jukebox plays George Jones
Or Johnny Cash or some new punk.

You know the routine like prison etiquette
And feel your shoulders tighten as they
Did after a spring start when everybody
Thought you were tough as a tractor.

They see you in here, Mr. Tough Guy
Back home from the game, back home
From luxury with that reputation
That painted you into beer commercials,
Sports columns right up to the demise.

They never want to know why you're here,
What you been doing since the rotator cuff.
It's a rugged yardstick,
But where else can you go?

NEW WHEELS

Full stride, between bases,
He's like a horse ungathering.

These swipes, a task
The gods gave to him,

In his impetuous dive,
Outstretching the frisky catcher's peg—

His lead, showing the tip
Of the iceberg of his bold heart.

Stop the sun; stop the moon;
You can't brake these new wheels.

FROM LONG DISTANCE, VIA THE EMAIL

A friend babbles on
About the general sorriness of the night,
The humidity in his neck of the state,
The wretched breakdown of our twisted society,
His poverty and the breach of his spirit,
America's innumerable sins and
The point blank presence of the devil
In our everyday lives,
Our very blindness to evil and greed.

He wants a comment on these poems,
That pound like Excedrin headache number 99
On my tired eyes, my neck that stiffens
From all the Saturday yard work and
The hard fouls my kids laid on me
While playing our vicious version of 21.

I write back, "Watch the Braves tomorrow.
They are black and white, Hispanic, rich and
Good. Their pitchers are smart, mannerly
And at times, intellectual. The manager is
Probably an alcoholic, the pitching coach rocks
Back and forth with Tourette's. Win or lose,
Night after night, it is a glorious affair,
It is better than snuff. Watch them, then
Write some more poems."

ON THE STREET IN ATLANTA, WALKING FROM ONE HOTEL TO ANOTHER

Talking to this tall, handsome black man
Who told me his little brother
Had been a major league ballplayer—
And he was thrilled because I remembered him,
A Phillie from the 70's,
I even recited his batting average
From the year he led the National—

Walking and dodging the breathless traffic,
He told me with a guarded kind of pride
How his brother and dad fought
Over college or baseball,
Their painful hard long arguments,
How the Phillies landed a helicopter
At a high school game
And flew that boy's heart away.

Up a hill, down a hill,
Walking through Atlanta,
He told me with a confidential wink
About Dick Allen at the house for dinner—
Allen smoking an existentialist cigarette
On the top step of the dugout,
Hanging his great potential
In the indifferent wind of Philadelphia boos.

Walking on carved out, once-burned streets
Of Atlanta, along the jugular, from one hotel to another,
Conjuring images of another, more exotic city
And a child's game that beckons few black men
Anymore
Above us, the fresh dark screen of Southern sky,
The last living witness to the conquering flames,
Waiting for the next thing.

LEARNING TO HATE THE METS

Here at the end of the "Braves Decade"—
And the Lord knows we paid our dues to have one—
A new challenge emerges called the Mets.

As a faithful follower of America's Team
Since they served their hospitality as
The doormat of the senior circuit,
It is now officially time to
Learn to hate the Mets.

It helps that I already didn't like them,
Or any team from New York, for that matter—
And with their off season shopping spree
And trading hysteria, I hardly know who they
Are, and that helps, too.

It is easier to hate a nameless beast, so
It's best to pay no attention to individuals
Like that pretty-boy catcher they stole
From the Dodgers last year—
I don't want to know about those pitchers
They procured at the fire sale, either.

I will learn to hate the sound of their name.
I will loathe their mention in the box scores at night.
I will think about them on a first grade level
When the world is still reduced to good and evil.
I will learn to hate this team that I already dislike
Without even trying.

You Feast on the Heat

120 on the field,
The air like the inside of a dryer—
The first inning is a struggle with placement
And a few weak ones get punched
Over the infield, one first-pitch blunder
Flies to the base of the Turner Field wall.
The crowd shifts uneasily.
It's the same story every year:
"Has the phenom lost his stuff?
We love him, but maybe there's
Still time for a trade."
Another sweaty inning—the four-
Run lead is cut in half.
The hard hitting Phillies
Go up and down twice as he
Mixes everything anywhere between
82 and 87: in, out, up, down,
Tailing, curving, dipping, floating—
It is so marvelous to watch,
And the whole universe seems to
Fit in the heat-inspired strike zone
While the Braves smash four home runs
And Maddux finally exits after seven
With a 12–4 lead, and the disbelievers
Have to hold off for one more game,
One more poker-faced contest of darts,
One more time for the smartest
Pitcher I've ever seen.

THE LITTLE BULLDOG

As much the defining image for an
Era as Hank and his lumberjack liners,
Pat Jarvis, toppling to the left side of
The Atlanta mound, after another
Ferocious effort at a fastball—Pat,
For several years the Opening Day
Hurler, when all that stood between victory
And certain defeat was the will of the
Little Bulldog.

Built like a prep school lineman, Jarvis worked
As fiercely, as boldly as a gladiator,
With a broken dam defense and the best
Hitting this side of the Bronx behind him,
He labored through legendary Atlanta
Dog days for seven years, then that misfire
In Montreal and out the tunnel and
The good-bye barrel of the game.

The Little Bulldog, who was after all,
Us out there on the hill, proving any
Man tough enough and willed enough could share
A mound with Niekro, McLain, Reed, even
Satch that one crazy summer. Seven years
Eighty-five wins riding Aaron, Cepeda,
Alou, Carty—aggressive bats all—
The Little Bulldog staked that rubber with
The clump of a heavy cleat. When I just
Started to watch and hear the games, he brought
Us all hope.

EVERY DAY

There is a high tight pitch—
Will you lean into it?
Set your wrists and swing
Like a September wind—
Will you recognize death
When it whistles
Under your chin?
Or reach for another cold one
Accidentally sparing
The slam of your head
And wondering what
That strange twitch
Of uneasiness
Might have been
As your heart burn
Clenches its ugly fist.
Every day
There is a high tight pitch—
Will you lean into it?

Tweener Days

When the heat lowers its indifferent cloak
And you have cold-showered the dog with the hose,
The ice cream box is empty and upside down
In the trash can, and your prescription for painkillers
Has finally run out;
When the wind is an annihilated memory,
The grass as crisp and brittle as insect shells—
These are the tweener days:
Sandwiches of death and dust
Between life and frothy fresh brew—
Tweener days
When I pull out a bucket of paint
Just to defend something I own,
When I plug up the radio in an outdoor socket
Just to apprehend a baseball game
With my parched imagination
While the garage doors smile with a new overcoat,
The pitcher labors and the whole
Sonorous, inviolable scene could
Split like a spilt jigsaw at any moment,
But doesn't
Because tweener days
Are only an alley, a valley betwixt
The old times
And a brand new set of unclocked ticks.

AUGUST 1920

The Cleveland shortstop leans in over the plate,
And the game will never be the same.
Carl William "Sub" Mays delivers a "submarine"
Fastball from so low it's like a viper striking
Up from the New York dirt,
Smacking Ray Chapman so hard at the temple,
His skull sounds like wood
Dulled by four months of contact,
And the fielders try to play it,
Like it came off the bat.
But Ray is already gone,
And the game will never be the same.
Hitters can thank Chapman
For a sacrifice that tipped the scales,
For clean white balls,
Hard plastic helmets,
Smaller strike zones.
And "Sub," he'd pitch nine more years,
Win 208, live 51 more seasons
Without the blame we somehow
Feel the need to give him.

In This Keen Light

Death, my Father, you cannot come here now—
You, who are the prize that waits at the bottom
Of the box, who would slam your lid on a
Struck batter, little more than child with
Downy, fuzzy cheeks. You, who were a fierce
Pitch in August of '20, cannot come here
Tonight, can not enter the white cement
Blocks of this basement to curl like a
Cat by my bare feet, not while I study
Whitman's white beard or write an ode to a
Long dead shortstop.

Death, my Father: do not think I cannot
Hear your rattle in the cold pipes that rise
From the harsh well of memory. You, who
Took my friends and left me like a bread crumb
Along this dark forest trail. Metaphors
Do not die easily, and Carl Mays
Pitched nine years with Chapman gone to the ground,
Lived another haunted forty-two,
Nearly illiterate, knowing that you
Are both foreshadow and shadow, that we
Live unaware in the keen light between.

THE INTRUSION OF SNAKES

I'm not talking simple temptation here—
Hunger facing the apple every day.
From the fake leather bible I left out
In the rain, I uncoiled this stiff lesson,
Rocking back and forth in hoarse rings of smoke.

Lucky are we who know the joy of
Simple sin, of yellowed fingers and hands
Shaky the next ugly day, who sleep all
Morning like smashed empty cans drifting in
Dull dreams—we who know not the intrusion,

The mad intrusion of snakes, oily voices
That send a ballplayer crawling up the backstop,
Writhing, squirming chemicals that twist the
Clock hands around the summit of the sad
Moon, the bad equation that stalks my friend
Sam, a poet, through a plague of hisses—
Who knows the fangs of paranoia
And the cold poison that leaves him
Gasping for reality.

What Can You Know About Donnie Moore?

Something about specialization,
Filing it all down to one focal point,
To where a given pitch can mar you—

So that nothing, the coke, the booze,
Can block the pain of everything rising—
And the day becomes an impossible challenge
Of keeping it all down.

Great literary guns once
Chose their own demise, in a trend
That approached a fictional kind
Of madness—

Had they slipped to the
One pony show of the closer,
Or felt it close at hand like
An already planned next chapter?

What can we know about Donnie Moore?
He hit no home runs,
He stole no bases
In thirteen seasons.
I watched him work hard in
Dale Murphy's Atlanta,
Then rise to greatness in Anaheim—
Till that critical moment in '89
When he knew better than God
What to do next.

SCIENCE FICTION

It is thought that travels
Faster than light,
Thought that smacks the pitch
That registers ninety-eight,
Thought that releases the springs
In the third baseman's leap,
That teases the pitcher with his fate
As the ball leaves his hand.

TEMPLE AMERICA

No time to smell
The leather of a stadium pitch—

You must earn
The stiff whiff of it,

Must make that mandatory
Extra call in your shiny sales shoes

Or in your natty golf mukluks
Or your too white tennis shorts.

No time to snatch the old glove,
Toss the back and forth with the kids,

Explain a hit and run,
The importance of backing up third—

You will pay coaches, good coaches
For these things.

There is a better and a better house
To think of,

The millionaire's club to make,
A hot vacation to shoot for—

No freaking time, no freaking time,
And the freeway
Is crowded
Like a pigsty
With your kind.

Waiting for Godot's Fly Ball

It is a beautiful day in center field:
The thick grass sports a dark emerald hue.
The ground is smooth, the sky is fair,
And a rumor has it a fly ball is on the way.

Wolfgang has tightened his track
Three hundred feet from home plate,
The place he is sure the ball will arrive.
Larson, who lingers in left, begins to drift

Lonely as a cloud to back up his compadre.
He calls out in a pleasant voice, "I am
Here, my brother. Do not be afraid;
I shall save you should you fail."

Wolfgang plops his big right hand
Into his glove thrice, then shields his delicate
Face from the splendid sun, "Bless you,
My dear brother," he calls out in a voice

Filled with confidence and just a hint of
World weariness. "I have not seen this
Fly ball yet, but I have heard that it is
A very high one indeed," he adds as

Larson stops just behind Wolfgang's protracted shadow.
"I fear the air is too thin, my friend; the ball
May grow eyes in this perfect sky."
"Come here beside me, my brother," Wolfgang's

Voice now deepened in sadness, "It is so lonely
Out here, even though the flight of the ball
Is imminent, and with it, the quickened pace of the game.
Come over here beside me, and let us wait together."

You Pitch the Night to Me

Your freeze-frame fastball fizzles
Like the wet blue fuse of me—

Your baneful curve curls from
A burning page in an open diary—

Your cool changeup waits for my cows to come in,
But my cows drink gin and refuse to come in—

Your furtive fork ball finds
The lies I hid behind a smile and a kiss—

As I leave the game quietly,
You record another strikeout.

♦ ♦ ♦ ♦

The Coach

He actually told his son this:
Go off somewhere
And kill yourself, okay?
His son he suspected of being gay
And found out,
His son he coached
Around the frangible bases
Of childhood,
His freckle-faced son he taught to hunt
Deer, rabbit, squirrels,
His spirited son he trucked to races
And pro baseball games—
His devoted son who played beside me
In the outfield
And later visited at college—
Who picked up my tab
More than I did his,
Who once told me he
Wanted to be a minister—

The coach, who, in the flame
Of heartless anger, actually told him this
Should not have been surprised
When his good son obeyed.

Needle in the Haystack at the Middle of the Week

These Wednesdays are the sword
You wrench from the stone.
You tap a cleat
On the top step of the dugout
And think about nothing.

A teammate pops you
In the side of the head
With his glove as he passes,
And you barely wince.

You watch the third base coach
As he fidgets and paces
And realize your wife
May be gone by the weekend—
There are signals, and then,
There are signals.

Lost in the middle of the bench,
You perch between the pitching coach
And the dopey trainer.

As the last long innings
Slouch by, you imagine what it would
Feel like to be found here

And returned to the first days
Of all the weeks when all that
Possibility loomed so sweetly
Like a promise to yourself
That you would never break.

How Can You Be Objective About a Trip to the Plate?

For the guy in Section 6 who screams at Crawdad batters

It's the hardest thing to do in all of professional sport—
Even Michael with all his quickness and style and
Absolutely supreme confidence failed and bailed—
Haven't you seen through those catcher cams,
The trail of something round and white?
Catch yourself next time, when the ash
Grows long on your cigarette and you pour
Another straight gin and call the second baseman
A no-hitting bum—Catch yourself,
Then go down to the nearest batting cage
Where you can watch a couple Single-A players
Dig in and swat that mechanical stuff.
Then you can mash a helmet
Down on top of the hurt that is your head
And step in with the bat you've still got
From Pony League days, a thirty-four inch
Louisville Slugger with a couple dents in it—
From where you hit rocks one night when
You had too much to drink and you felt
A strong summons to your glory days—
Step in with the machine set to maximum
(It probably peaks at 80),
See how objective it feels when the bat
Stings your soft hands
When you're lucky and swift enough
To even make contact.
Next, buy another round of swings
And reduce the speed to 60.
You may find you're ready for
Little League pitching,
Which might be an objective experience
For a thirty year old man.

MAKING THESE WORDS FOR YOU

Try to find work after forty
When you look like a used up boxer
And your reputation is spread
Through the rolling county hills
Like the split paint of you—
Till finally the only work you *can* get
Is store clerk where everyone
Can witness your fall
And exploit you as an example
For their gutless depraved children.
I can hear the bearded, cap-wearing men
In their red super cab pickups,
Telling their teenaged progeny,
"Why, I remember when that guy
Was the captain of the high school
Baseball team, best pitcher we
Ever seen, but the dope and the licker
Got him—That could be you Billy,
Susie, Ronald, Heather, Jeffrey, Todd."

Living like this is much too skinny—
I was supposed to be fat rich,
Cigar-smoking successful—
Wear fine suits with a trophy wife
Out volunteering, a house at the beach,
Overachieving kids.
I live in a garage apartment
Behind a stone house
Once owned by, of all things,
A boilermaker.
I watch the family that occupies the house:
The children are bright-faced
Little ghosts of what my kids once were—
They tumble and skip around the backyard—
They have a trampoline there.

Through the window behind the tube
I watch like Boo Radley,
See a head, a set of shoulders—
Do they wonder about me? if I'm some
Boogey man, a pale-faced skinny guy
That only seems to leave for work
Then return grayer than the lost light
Of evening?
Have they been told that I am a coach
That lost everything—the job, the family,
The future?
That I am trying hard to get over the need
To kill, for retribution,
My hatred of God and fortune?
I stir my brandy with a nail and forget
All the winning faces,
The championship embraces.
I sit here with a low heart
And all the long lost hope of this fall—
Making these words for you.

Half-Talent

"I know that there is nothing more incomplete than a half-talent; a man should either be a genius or nothing at all."—Charles Bukowski

To be almost at the top
Is the thing that drives you most crazy;
To find that last step too steep,
That final echelon of opposition too tough;
To make the AAA and do well
But have that All-Star ahead in the Bigs—
To look up with a gaze of wonder
At the soles of his fabulous feet,
And sigh through a September of false hope
And fight through a winter of indecision.
And all along think that if you had turned
Your stance a little this way or that
Somewhere in your ascension,
That you could be there,
The burgeoning rookie—
Ah, to be almost at the top
Is the thing that drives you over the edge.

THE OUTLAW PETE ROSE

Slinks down a minor league runway,
Hawk-eyes the prospects,
Shouting an illegal speech
Toward the stunned outfielders.
The stadium attendant
Tells the head groundskeeper,
"Pete's a good guy, really."
The outlaw Pete Rose views
The one-third of the field
He's allowed to see, the sacks
He reached over four thousand times
Are hidden by railing and concrete.
His profile is tanned granite
Turning like a jet turns
Away from a city.

Somewhere the horses are running
And an old man measures
Hoofbeats and heartbeats,
An old man, doomed by perfect vision.

Pete Haunts the Real Fans Like the Ghost of Baseball Past

He wants it as bad as he ever wanted to bat
With the bases loaded, the game on the line,
The deciding contest of a seven game Series.

To sit at the end of a bench and hold a lineup card
With major league names on it,
To send that raw rookie into the cage and
Show him how to keep the front leg straight,
To swing not from the heels but with eyes
Tuned to the turn of the seams,
To make the pitching change that intuition suggests,
To pinch hit against the percentages,
To hit and run and hit behind runners—
To teach them all of it, head first, plain and simple,
The way the game oughtta be played.

♦ ♦ ♦ ♦

I will write about you, Pete,

Just like you hit,
All these short little poems:
Singles stroked just over the infield,
Choppers with eyes for the middle,
Some nights daring to take
That extra base, the outfielder
Lulled by the rhythm of an August game.

I will lay the pipe of this story,
Measured section by section
Into seasons that link together
As my opus of testimony
For your Hall of Fame trial.
I will write about you, Pete.

At the plate, Pete,

Your head turned like an owl's—
The focus on the ball so complete
You saw the dust jump from the mitt
When the slider inched off the corner.

Your eyes stopped short
Of the umpire's face most of the time,
But the bat that wagged, then sagged
Level with the delivery was all that mattered
To the hardest hitter to strike out
Ever—

◆ ◆ ◆ ◆

Why do we leave Pete

Out there on the bases,
Pacing off and back to the bag,
Plotting to take third on his own
If he has to,
Eyeing the sneaky shortstop
Across his right shoulder
Which he slightly dips,
Gathering a little loose dirt
In his hands, thinking about third,
But always his heart on home?

Why do we leave Pete out there?
The last duck from his particular pond,
Scratching his head and remaining
Focused on third, trying hard to
Forget about the effort that
Got him to second?
Why do we leave Pete out there?
And will he stay till the lights go out?
Will he dance in the sprinklers
As the moon slowly rides across the sky?
Why do we leave him out there?

PETE, TO PLAY LIKE A RELENTLESS FORCE,

It's something you rarely see these days.
When average fellows cultivate
Palatial estates overlooking the nights
And the cities where they sign their hearts,
Supposedly.

But who plays like a relentless force?
Who runs out the walks and sprints
The bases, regardless—?
Who runs over a catcher in an All-Star Game?
Who returns to the dugout
Where he can't sit still?
Needles and Wheedles the umps
And the other team,
Would coach third base
If they'd let him,
Whose head first slides
Could be the most compelling image
Of an era of great ball-playing?

I ask you, Pete,
Who goes to war between the lines
"Relentless as the tarantula"?

THE BEST THING ABOUT BASEBALL

Is that there are so many games.
Hot, cool, warm, and rainy nights,
Days when the nerves
Throw the pine to the fire—
Vacant days when you
Can't remember getting dressed
Or who's in town.
The long season is a catalyst
For ritual: where you stand
During the anthem, where
You sit in the dugout or the pen,
The place you touch your cap
Before you step in the box—
The way you look first at your
Left shoe, then your right
As you settle for the pitch—
The pocket in which you
Keep the chew you never chew.
Sometimes it boggles your
Mind when you think that
You are only a cog of the
Greater wheel of ritual
As you work on the liturgy
That you sing to the batter
From your holy position
At third base.

Too many good things at once

Strike fear into the slugger—
A triple crown season,
The birth of a third child, a son,
The doting love of a beautiful woman
And parents that give and give
Though he's already got and got.

He carries the clover—you know the one—
In his first baseman's mitt,
Practices the Spanish it takes
To communicate with the other infielders
And the catcher;
Everyone wants a commercial, it seems,
Though he can't begin to act,
In fact sounds and looks like
A nervous mule when the camera rolls.

It is what he's worked for since he was six,
When he was given this easy, natural game
Without hoops or goals or fouls or penalties.
But now the pit of his stomach tells him
About the other foot—
Death creeping or maiming injury.
Too many good things, he thinks,
And secretly buys more insurance,
Notices how the clover dries faster
And must always be replaced,
The four leaves growing harder
And harder to find.

After Johnson's Mother Died

It was like living
With the remnants of a hurricane,
A rug flipped up and gritty around the edges,
A curtain pulled open to the side of the window
Smudged with cat nose prints—
Where he stared out the hours
Hoping to catch what would creep
Around the brick corner,
What crazy eyes would insert themselves
Into every wind-blown pair of loops.

A pair of lost earrings lay
In a dusty den corner
By the kids' old wooden rocking horse—

Johnson's third base stealing foot tapped
To the soundless television—
His home run hitting arms tightened
As he clung to the arms that held him,
The arms of his favorite chair.

Somewhere Out There

Beyond the rim of what we can see,
A drain waits for Mantle's uncareful foot—
A drain named Martin moves in slow
Pickup truck movements across
The hoary crest of the morning hill.
Somewhere out there,
History loops in long horse lopes
As Davey Lopes covers second
On a runaway steal.
Somewhere out there,
Time staggers on the teeth of a reel
And the God of the universe
Checks His counter obsessively
And curses quietly to Himself.

WHAT DOES HE KEEP IN HIS BAG?

The slugger keeps something in his bag,
The dark green canvas one that he lugs
To practices and games alike, carrying
His glove separately and his cap on his head
And his cleats already laced tightly.
There is something else that he keeps
In the bag that sits with him on the bench,
That he places carefully in the corner
When he takes the field and checks it
First when he clomps back in.

Everyone has seen him unzip
The long zipper across the top and
Reach inside for something, then pull
His huge hand back without powder
On it or anything sticky. When
Whatever it is moves around, it does
Not create the bulging straight lines
Of books or notebooks. From the way
He carries the bag, it does not appear
To be heavy; in fact, several players
Have discreetly checked the weight,
Jiggling it like a Christmas present.

The slugger is friendly, even to rookies,
And earns his magnanimous salary
Over and over, but he has this green
Canvas bag with something in it
That worries us all.

ALLOWED TO TRAVEL BACK IN TIME

Where would I go?
Why back to the sonorous days of school
When I had no lines for the girls,
When the games weighed more
Than my nerve to play them
And I rattled through an afternoon
With no love for science
Or the absolutes that teachers
Set before us?

Back to cleats clacking across
The cracked sidewalk
And down to the rough grass
Of the diamond that funneled
Out across the gridiron?
A stadium with no bleachers
Where you played to prove
Nothing and everything
To the few parents in frayed
Lawn chairs and to the occasional
Muscle car that rumbled
By in gravel parking lot blasting
The new Lynyrd Skynyrd, "Sweet
Home Alabama," or Joe Walsh's
"Rocky Mountain Way"?

There was a name for the condition
Of being hung out in that country school,
A name I can't recall—the same way
The ball now feels wrong in my grip—
In a scene where manhood
Is confirmed or not,
A scene not quickly forgotten—

Why would I go back?
Why, to run away from what all
IT got me, and, of course,
To make it all right
Once and for all.

This Edge That We Make, This Day That We Promise

There is a feeling that lines our pockets
That warms our hands securely, and saves us
From the corner where the grass lies under
The whirling mower blade, the green and brown
And white place where we make our edge against
The outside forces that rule this day, that
We promise away. And we live along
The drawn line, pitch to the black border of
The plate, check our swings against the deep urge
Of our groins, against the tired groans that
Would unmake us if we kept the promise
Of the day, the promise to cross the lines
To smash the glass that in silence holds us.

◆ ◆ ◆ ◆

Fumbling for This Thing Called Understanding

You caught me off base
With that critical blow, that smooth
Lack of tact, so tacitly maintained
Until—your eye locked me perfectly
In the scope and your voice froze me
Like the first distant rumbling
Of spring thunder beyond us
In the blue hills where we once
Hiked to rocks and towers
To see where we are now.
I swear I was not even stealing,
Even thinking of another base;
See my puzzled face in the picture,
The nervous way I held my hands,
Off base, but not so false
As to have you squeeze that trigger.

WHEN ONE GATE SHUTS

Another opens.
Just as a new day
Weaves its shadow
Across the soft infield,
Your heart courses with
The same blood that is
Different as tomorrow's clouds
And you're past second base
In this game you were born to play,
This metaphor that is
Now your blood, the flesh
Of your written word,
And nothing more holy
Than a gate that opens
And waits for you
On a glorious and powerful morning
Just like this.

Waiting for Some Power to Descend

His plastic lounger bent like a reverse
Radical sign, he hoists the alum-
inum cylinders, the swinging arm of
An oil drill—southpaw, as Dad always said,
Closer to first; with the weaker righty
He daubs foam from a peppery fringe of
Beard

Then fingers the pistol in his pocket,
While the radio fades and rises which
Makes no sense to Willie since the damned thing
Sits still against a tree root, and some car-
Pet-bagging Yankee crackles the Braves game
Between commercials and endeavors to
Furnish his half-witted opinion
About every cranny of the game.
Willie remembers the new ball, fresh
In his left hand at the start of an
Inning, watches the lake beyond his yard
For a tomato eating muskrat to
Swim within range across the murky bilge
That once drew him to this spot like a
Divining rod. Now the sunset is
Unnatural, houses and roads edging
From all sides, his world slowly coming
To a stagnant end—in a ninth inning

As the bases load with Reds and a hungry
Muskrat raises its sneaky head, he sets
Down the beer and calls forth the pistol,
Sighting down the barrel through bifocals.
The radio fans roar across the waves
And Willie knows that only Rocker and a bullet can
Save this precious day.

Horsehide on the Waves— Romancing the Channel

There is the stalwart, aged fishing boat,
The gnarled old fisherman—white hair
Reddened skin, gravelly voiced with a
Farmer's barbed wire temper—an honest,
Simple man, sixty-year-old muscles
As taut as the steel cables on the trawlers
Which pass him going out, as he must,
Three days at a time with a wicked grandson
And a pampered nephew as a crew.
They fight the sun, the roiling waves,
An untidy storm or two, and fish.
At night as the boat rocks in anchored rhythm,
The Red Sox come in on a radio wave;
They are cursed like he is, to never land
The big one, to live on the spare hope
Of another year. When he started out here
There was Williams, the best there ever
Was—and the best there ever will be—
Worth two Babe Ruths, he tells those punks;
Then there was Yaz and Tony C,
Rice and Lynn, and finally this bunch
They got now—this cocky bunch.
Light gales of wind slap the old boat
With white caps. The familiar fisherman
Prays a silent prayer for the Sox
As the radio signal slowly bleeds
Out of range in the bottom of the seventh.

ACROSS FROM HUFFMAN BALLPARK

Where Little League champions are bred
Trained, and toughened,
There is Hawksridge Nursery, where acres
Upon acres of green houses brim with lush
Plants, shrubs and trees.
Behind the gigantic nursery, the owner keeps
A pasture for buffalo, his special passion.

The buffalo are big, sweet, domestic animals.
Not bred to be champions, they receive
No training like the Little Leaguers
So last week when someone cut a hole
In the pasture fence, four of the dark beasts
Wandered off into the community.

They are humble in their own way,
But cannot be taught to run the bases—
And if they could be, you would not
Want to block one from the plate;
In fact, they cannot particularly be told
Where to go, hence the fence

So farmhands, finding two in a peach grove
A couple hundred yards behind our house
Shot them. Two down.
One wandered on its own back into the pasture
Perhaps at the rumor of the shootings.

A highway patrol cruiser encountered
The fourth one at three in the morning
As it crossed State Highway 127
And sent it to buffalo heaven.

Now the neighborhood's back to normal,
The fence mended, the champions back
In school, and we're still the same sad
Animals making our way through
The dull days of August, killing whatever
Dignity escapes the barriers we have built.

WHEN THE HORN CALLS THE HAMMER

For Henry Aaron

At the factory whistle's insistence
In the first high layer of yellow dusk,
A pistol rings against the silence

For a game that was played in the rapt hush
Of a century that, hand over mouth,
Held truth back in its gray cancerous breath,

For a quiet man that rose above the
Courtesies that asserted the levels
Across the plane of play and picked the fruit,

Peeled, ate and forgot the visceral mean-
ing of the tree, making the man a non-
man, a quiet man for whom the horn blooms

Its flowers of sweet reverberation.
The horn calls the hammer into mansions
Of fanfare, blown kisses, recognition
And finally peace.

A MYTH BEFORE THE BIRTH, MANTLE

Already a myth before the birth of
His career, Mantle hit the shots that "stayed
Hit," as the fans flocked and cameras flamed
In the dry Arizona sun, stunned by the
Thrack of his connection. Hall of Famers
Tried to remember a similar sound
But couldn't. That one at USC, thought
Near six hundred feet, and Mick under six
Himself, admitted he'd never seen a
Shrimp till his teammates ordered. Mick, whose three
Point one to first saved him from the zinc and
Lead mines. Mick, who would play as injured as
A rodeo cowboy, gored by drink
And a good time, knees mummified at
Thirty-two, whose career like his cleats got
Stuck in the drain, ruined and praised by Stengel.
Dead, buried and resurrected like
Any good drunk, in for the next hand of
Cards, out like a meal whose taste you can't
Remember.

◆ ◆ ◆ ◆

PEPI PLAYED THE GAME LIKE A TUNE

Pepi played the game like a tune you can't
Get out of your head, a sweet melody
That bridged the gaps between innings, beyond
The xylophone of games, into the fissures
Of dark nights that linger like missing teeth.
After the jazz had settled into the
Taxi horns of a bright New York affair,
Pepi played precociously, a different
Tune as often as he could, by sunlight
Crossing the chalk to his guardhouse at first,
By the evening thinking of where the lights
Might take him. Every swing a whole note—
Miss or hit—Pepi played the game like a tune.

DROWNING LESSONS

The poet paused long enough for me to clear
A stopped-up ear, to kick off a tight shoe,
Then he poured the poem through the phone, began
Reciting awards, elite reading engagements,
The posh smart people who'd squeezed his hand, the
Winks from wives and girlfriends, hitchhiking
Back when America was still "something"
To see—education, not yet so hollowed,
When smart cookies like him struggled to win,
"The truth" their only armament, rebels
Of a kind no one can fathom these days.
The poet paused long enough for me to switch
To my autopilot of grunts and *Yeah,*
*I know what you mean*s. While the opulence
Of ego raged on, I thought of a
Poor black kid from Mobile, toting great blocks
Of ice on his back, batting cross-handed
On the segregated playgrounds that would
Launch him, about the same time this poet
Was doing all his hard-time white-boy
Stuff, dedicating his very soul to art.

THE GENIUS OF GROWING OLD

Life is always pitching from the stretch, with
No reliever warming and waiting in
The pen: Can you keep those bills close to the
Base? Are you surrounded by bungling fielders?
Or a catcher who can't quite get it done?

Life is always pitching from the stretch, glancing
With one eye across your shoulder at
Kids who will lapse or not lapse into dope
Or losing if you forget they're on board
For a minute, or at a wife you please

With unfinished attention when you can.
You are on the mound, you are leaning toward
The plate, you are reaching for the sky with
A wild kick at the stars; and the runners
In your stomach are forever moving
With the pitch.

UNCLE JOHN VISITS

Uncle John likes the Yankees, rubs it in
Each year they destroy the Braves. My dad,
His younger brother, likes the Tigers, but
They have been a long time nothing to talk
About. When John and Aunt Helen come up
From Salisbury for lunch and an afternoon,
I stop by to chat, to hear John and Dad
Despise Republicans and brag about the
Grandkids. John's ahead on ballplayers, like
Those Yankees in October—he is just
Matter-of-fact about his "star pitcher."

Uncle John is not the smooth talker that
Dad is. He rubs his hand across his
Pencil of mustache, clears his throat and starts
In a voice an octave higher than
His little brother's, "I b'leve the
Yankees'll come around," clears his throat
Twice more, "about October or so," and
He nods his head to agree with himself.

Dad's bald head trembles slightly like when he's
About to deliver the first line of
A prayer or a sermon, and he clears his
Throat authoritatively and begins,
"The Braves are definitely better this
year than those Yankees, built from scratch, too," he
adds, implying something rotten about
New York. And so it goes until they get
Back to despising Republicans or
I get ready to leave, whichever comes
First.

COCOON

At lunch, I watch
My Dad move further toward the middle O.
He reclines with lunch,
A hand on the remote control,
A loaded shotgun propped
Against the stool next to his chair.
He is seventy-three, the man
Who caught a hundred thousand
Of my pitches and taught me
When to throw them.
He has automatic deposit and payment
On everything possible, a German Shepherd
Chain-fenced against his carport.
He has gained weight
Since "licking" cancer and hopelessly
Watches his diet.
He has cable TV and the Braves pitchers
"Are not getting the calls this year."
He loved that slow curve and had me
Work till I threw it with a fastball delivery.
He rides instead of drives now, mornings
He is chaplain at the Lutheran Home,
Ministers to the sick and the lonely.
There and back he goes
And the circle grows smaller.
"There's a squirrel in my cherry tree,"
He tells me, "And I'm going to get it."
I finish my own soup,
Try not to look at the shotgun.

IF WE ALL GAVE IN TO CONVENTION

we'd have no Fydrich, no mad Hrabosky
squared behind the mound to face his Buddha.

Dizzy would bore us, Yogi, correct us.
Denny and Pete certainly bet less.

Where might we be without Lefty or
the Spaceman, or the smiling ghost of Satch?

Leo rocks while Rocker fidgets and coils.
Everybody spits; sometimes, somebody
hits.

MORE BASEBALL HAIKU

I.

Blue silver moonlight
On orange field, pumpkins
Night before the Series

II. The Earth Fields Everything

Burst of cadmium
Leaves toppling and toppling
In uncertain arcs

III.

Ragged gloves, a ball
Through snow the father and son,
A mound and plate thawed

♦ ♦ ♦ ♦

ONE NIGHT AT LP FRANS

After the Crawdads game
On a cool June night with a breeze,
The great used car giveaway occurs.
Five luxury autos—count them
As they enter and park on the runway
Behind home plate.
The crowd, usually fighting its way
Toward exits, is wild with excitement;
There's more anticipation than during
The Domino's Pizza scream, or the
Wild scuffle and scurry as the stadium
Attendants catapult rolled up t-shirts
Into the fray.

One by one the geek from the car lot
Pulls a name and waits for a human form
To descend the concrete steps to sign
A title on the spot and drive that creampuff
Into the darkness of the night.

My fifteen-year-old silently calculates
Our/his chances—a thousand or so lingerers
Versus two entries. He slouches with what's
Left of his drink as a drunk comes bouncing down
From the top bleacher, jumping and yelling
Like Fred Flintstone, only to stop at the
Box seats to admit his lie.
The geek says to put the scoundrel
On the black list and proceeds with
The final drawing, one for a white Dodge
Something or another with a burned out
Headlight. Not a bad vehicle, really—but
Then there's that name again that's
Not mine or Penny's, and everybody scatters
To the parking lot where they left
The cars and trucks for which they sweated,
The ones the banks own, or the leasing agencies.

Moments later, we're in the Red Taurus
Trying to leave—when there blocking
the exit is the brown generic car, the smoker
That barely wanked it this far before dying
We all double up in laughter
In one of those truly great family moments,
At the kind of irony on which
A family must survive.

The Deep End of Dog Days

You scowl and blather and teeter when it's
Mostly a matter of sleep, when the dry
Air gathers and separates visibly,
The bear walks and the camel runs for the
Well and you reach for the unexpected
Perfection of memory that lingers
Like an old song—August, and deep in the
Count, the uneasy feeling of slipping
Like a recording down the chart, but this
Is a game, a sport with black and white
Conclusions, nothing so sudden as fame
That strays to unadjusted fools elsewhere.
A pitch is a pitch even on the black
Edges of a waiting plate—the eyes
Perceive, the wrists expand, the bat misses
Even as your memory projects the
Sphere into its precise orbit.

◆ ◆ ◆ ◆

Who Could Forget

Who could forget a
Bright saffron moon just beyond
The left fielder's reach

EACH MORNING

I watched
The old couple fast-walk their paved driveway,
Brisk in dark jeans, light jackets.
He wore a Yankees ball cap, she a black scarf;
They looked happy, energetic in their constancy,
A near-strut to and from the bustling highway
Where sputtering cars sloughed toward work,
Drivers, red-faced over sloshing coffee.
Some, indifferent, cigarette-lipped with
Burning, growling stomachs paid the couple
No attention.

A protracted winter passed while I drove
Another route to a different job.

Today I travel the old way past their house.
I watch the old man,
Notice a new leanness to his face,
The red perk vanished from his cheeks,
The lift absent from his stride,
His baseball cap missing.
He walks alone.

In Outlaw Tales

For Hank Utley (Co-Author of The Carolina Independent
  Baseball League, 1936–38*)*

Digging through these pages of young faces
Of the old and the dead I never knew,
Of hard stories of men with bleak futures
When the elevator of order had
Snapped a cable and sent good people swan
Diving from windows in busted cities
And baseball was a fizzled firework fuse
Stomped all but out, all but these mad outlaws.

In Carolina mill towns where fans dressed
In Sunday best on a Wednesday afternoon,
The women in hats, the men ready to
Fight the rabble from across the county:
Kannapolis and Concord, Valdese
And Hickory, Lenoir and Shelby. The
Hard, depressed pride on the line with ringers
Stolen from minor and major league teams—
College boys and gritty veterans,
The innocent and the aged, come to
The call of the civic dollar, and the
Winter work at the mills—outlaws, red-cheeked
Boys blacklisted and footloose in this
Moveable feast of bendable rules
Where names changed and five bucks a week could send
A man fifty miles up or down the same
Road twice in one season—boldly nicknamed
Heroes like "Struttin" Bud Shaney; "Razzy"
Miller, an ordained minister; "Alabama"
Pitts, a paroled convict. I am

Digging through these pages of young faces,
The benevolent mill owners, whose utter
Influence stretched further than their stockings,
Dapper men who knew their people demanded
More than bread, water, and bible—men more
Bold than one would ever guess, outlaws: church
Deacons and councilmen. I think of Mark
Bolick, who put an arm on my shoulder,
Fresh from college, urged me toward the cloth—

An outlaw, vice-president of the league—
So proud to know a name that comes speaking
Off these pages against my fixed memory.
Outlaw memories:
Tales of balls weighted with phonograph needles;
Fences blocked by shrubbery, balls stashed under
For the home field advantage; prospects convinced
By money at a train stop to stay for
A wild week of games—the untold gambling
In a country that seemed to have no future
Beyond the first call of the next train whistle.

The tired, hungry eyes of dusty-footed
Children, gathered for a game under a
Southern sun: "I'm Barton, I'm Hitchner..."
As trucks filled with soft cotton roll in and
Out of town—while the lunch whistle at the
Mill calls rough-handed men to a sandwich,
Outlaws stretch stories across the lusty
Looms of memory.

KITCH

Is a crazy old guy at the rest home
Who leans over the arm of his lounger
And spits, his empty jaw puffed with a chaw
Of invisible tobacco, then with
Both hands, adjusts his burgundy cap
And tells me to just try that curve again.

Uncle Jack says that a long time ago
Kitch played, was a career minor leaguer,
A local celebrity who never
Got the big break, yet wouldn't let go,
Into his forties, on the bottom rung.

"Come here, come here," he says to me, startling
Blue eyes locking on my skeptical face.
"They're changing the signs again, I swear they
Are," his voice breaking. "They're still the same,
Kitch, still the same," I assure him. "One more
Thing, just one more thing," his voice lowers,
Signaling me to come closer; "Did I,
Did I make it? Did I make it?" Softer
This time, "Of course you did, Kitch. Of course
You did. You're in there with the Babe."

Aunt Lucille

As we get older we will shake the dust off
Our shoes and walk into the picture like
Ghosts from the corn field and you will hear the
Call of our boyish voices through
The open kitchen window where you watch
The pattern of the game beyond the clothesline
And the flap of grandpa's overalls in
The soft August wind. We will play by the
Rules of the land till our sweat turns gray in
The evening—you will think of us later
From a bed in a rest home as the light
Dims slowly and you are floating, floating
Back home to the farm.

The Incense of Your Praise

For Penny

Before you, I was on-deck my whole life,
Stupid and always preliminary
To a better, faster opponent that
Played the game beyond my simple level.

Before you, I wandered the aimless field
Of misjudged flies, misplayed liners, a fist
Full of overthrown illusions, of unplanned
Fifth inning surrenders, forfeited time,
Even caught stealing once, slapped silly more.

Now I look back at the team we have built
Through the years of struggle, winning, losing
Sometimes, as the deck of days reshuffles.
I wait, undeserving for the blue moon
Only you can raise, the only one that counts.

Coming to the End of Things

For Ernie Johnson, Sr., September 22, 1999

Nothing stares at you
Like the blank page of another day,
So you fill them with conversation
And cards for the long flights
To the inevitable "coast"
Which long ago ceased
To look like another world
As you first thought,
First thought when you were a "kid"
Pitching relief for the Braves,
And the world of New York
Had been sold
For this soul-less land.

Now
The microphone is your
Comfortable pen, your
One-haired brush,
The exit door of your soul—
It has forked you out
To the rocking chairs and recliners
Of America—
Through the air,
Through the ground,
Beamed off the held up umpire's hands
Of satellites
You can barely imagine.

All that insider knowledge,
All that calm demeanor
Bordering on sweetness
In a game that eats it—
Surviving on the hope
That these last ten years
Would happen in Atlanta,
And when they did, still
Holding the glee right
At the surface, and even
In this final game, in this
Pennant race heat, closing
Familiarly, as he would only have it,
"On a winning night from Atlanta,
So Long."

Index